<u>NO! looking back</u>

I0145376

You'll Never Fall Again

By Nicholas Timmon

PART ONE OF THE BOOK SERIES

DESTINY'S FINEST HOUR

ISBN 978-0-6151-7993-3

All bible quotations are directly from the King James Version.

Distributed by lulu.com

Log on to **iapworldwide.org** for upcoming publications…

All glory to God the Father. All thanks to Christ Jesus my Lord, and King.

Special thanks to my wife Jennifer Nicole who inspired me to complete this project, and became the invigoration behind my dreams…

Table of contents:

"No looking back"

Her career as a high school track star reached its zenith. It was her senior year when she finally reached the one event that eluded her for so long; the track and field state championships. It was profuse preparation that brought her to this long desired destination. On the contrary, the results of this anticipated event would startle everyone while leaving a permanent residue. Ginger arrived ready, focused, and determined to win. She carried a rare swagger and confidence that resounded piercingly. Ginger was considered somewhat of an underdog seeing that she hadn't totally dominated in past events, but today would be different. The surreal look in her eyes nearly guaranteed a victory.

The spirit of competition saturated the air, and the hope of success filled the clear blue skies of rural South Georgia. Mr. Baron Ginger's track and field coach gave the entire team a motivating pep talk. Mr. Baron was bias to Ginger, because he also relished this long awaited day for her. He knew that she could exceed expectations, if she remained focused. Her coach was well aware that all the ingredients of a winner were within her. She was born to run baring long legs that took strides like a gazelle. Adversity was her friend not her foe, both on, and off the field. The challenge of being a singularity fueled her to be the best. It wasn't easy being one of the extremely few African Americans in her school, and the entire county for that matter. At the time rural South Georgia hadn't reached its peak of social equality. Nevertheless her athletic abilities were undeniable, and ranged from a diversity of sports. But track and field was the sport that she loved most, which is why winning at the state championships would validate her in more than one way.

The tensions were high during warm-ups, but they were about to escalate many decimals. The mental psyching process was over, it was time for action. Ginger competed in diverse events, but today the feature event would be the hurdles. With a slight bounce she eagerly approached the starting blocks. She quickly eyed her competition while confidently rubbing her hands together. With only a matter of seconds before the starting gun would sound, she once more stretched her quadriceps and hip flexors. She was determined to leave no room for mechanical error. Dawned in her schools scarlet red and glossy white uniforms she crouched down into her starting position. She immediately possessed tunnel vision, no one else existed. Bang! The starting gun rang. All the runners shot out at a frantic pace. Ginger remained parallel with the front runners. She approached her first hurdle and easily galloped over it landing in stride. She remained among the front runners through the second hurdle. Upon the third hurdle she exploded to take the lead by a couple of links. By the fifth she became reminiscent of Seattle Slew, alone and out front. Her pace was so fast she shocked her self. To her baffling, she noticed no one was within her reached. She knew that she was good, but couldn't conceive within her self being good enough to literally blow her competition away, especially at this level. Then came the moment that would change everything. Clearly surprised at her lead up to that point, she figured something had gone wrong with the functioning of the race, or thought maybe all her competition strangely disappeared? So she decided while in the lead and nearing the finish line to "look back" and see what was going on. The moment her head hit the 70 degree angle mark, everyone began passing her like a car on the high way would pass a bicycle. She lost a race that she had already won, only because she took a second to look behind her.

It is a redundant occurrence that each time a person who is liberated and moving forward from something that caused them detriment; that the moment they look back inquisitively, they are totally dismantled. The physical act of looking back such as turning your head is not what brings about ruin. The demise comes when you reminisce with passion on your past state of bondage. Don't get caught up in what I call the "how, and why syndrome." Just learn to accept favor instead of asking twenty questions. You will never understand <u>why</u> God decided to deliver you, even though you felt you didn't deserve it. Or <u>how</u> he delivered you, when you never seen where it came from. Accepting deliverance is the number one reason many are not delivered.

For something to be considered the past, you must have passed by it. We determine our own fate. The bible speaks of a story in the book of Genesis, about a city called Sodom and Gomorrah. This city was referred to as being wicked and full of vile affections. The debaucheries of this city displeased God so until he decided to destroy it along with everyone within it. One man named Lot found favor with God, because he did not participate in the immorality of Sodom and Gomorrah. God sent His angels to warn Lot of the destruction to come. The angels instructed him to take his wife, and his two daughters and escape to the mountains. The angels further instructed Lot and his family upon their exit to "look <u>not</u> behind" them. Remember an angel is a messenger of God Almighty so you must obey their orders. The angels led Lot and his family out of the city. Once Lot and his family were clear of the city God rained down fire and brimstone from heaven, and overthrew Sodom and Gomorrah, and its surroundings. In curiosity Lot's wife looked back to witness the destruction. She immediately became a pillar of salt.

When you disobey God's instructions, you are volunteering for destruction. The word freedom means to be exempt from bondage. Why continue to live in what nearly killed you in the first place? Before you pray to be delivered, you should want to be delivered. If being bound with calamity is what makes you happy, so be it. But if freedom is what you desire, receive it. Jesus Christ has claimed the victory for you. Through him you possess the title deed to your victory. Through Jesus Christ you are; undefeatable, you are rich, healed, and you are saved. As long as you continue to walk according to the Word of God and by the leading of the Holy Ghost, your future is destined for perfection. Run far away from your sins and all entanglement. Be assured that God has forgiven you. Never, ever look back with care of whence you come from. Only use your past lifestyle as a testimony of God's mercy, favor, and love. You are not what you used to be, but you are on your way to what God created you to be. Read the following passages of this book and adhere to its instructions, and don't look back.

Introduction

The second epistle of Peter, the first chapter verses four through ten reads:

4. *Whereby are given unto us exceedingly great promises:*
That by these ye might be partakers of the divine nature,
having escaped the corruption that is in the world through lust.
5. *And besides this, giving all **diligence,** add to your **faith virtue**;*
*And to your virtue **knowledge***
6. *And to your knowledge **temperance**; and to your temperance*
***Patience**; and to your patience **godliness**;*
7. *And to godliness **brotherly kindness**; and to brotherly kindness **love.**
8. *For if these things be in you and abound, they make you that ye shall neither be barren nor unfruitful in the knowledge of our Lord Jesus Christ.*
9. *But he that lacks these things is blind and cannot see afar off, and hath forgotten that he was purged from his old sins.*
10. *Wherefore the rather, brethren give diligence to make your calling and election sure:*
For if ye do these things, **ye shall never fall...**

The most distinct ability possessed by mankind is the power to fail, or succeed. There is a recipe for success; it is walking in the Spirit and living according to the Word of God. There also is a recipe for failure; it is living in disobedience to the Father and according to your vile natural desires. To succeed or accomplish something you must give an asserted effort, but to fall or fail at something takes no effort at all. It would seem that a creation which was created in the image of perfection (which is God) would possess no ability to disappoint in any way. No human has proven to be perfect as of yet. Even angels are not perfect, proven by Lucifer who was perfect in beauty and ways, until iniquity was found in him *(Ezekiel 28:15)*. Lucifer was referred to as perfect according to his outer workmanship. In Lucifer God created a perfected utensil for worship. Lucifer did make the first initial fall to be recorded which took place before the creation of man. He recognizing his flawless shell became puffed up with pride, and foolishly thought that he could over throw the Almighty God. He was immediately kicked out of heaven along with one third of its occupancy (angels) that he had persuaded, which are now considered demons. Lucifer once the anointed cherub, is now Satan (the accuser), or can be referred to as the devil.

The next immeasurable fall would be by man or Adam. Man was created in the image of God and was given total dominion over the earth, and all its inhabitants. Man was given specific instructions, "do not partake of the tree of knowledge of good and evil or you will surely die." Adam using his unique ability of will chose to disobey God. Adam ate of the tree despite God's specific instructions, after being persuaded by woman to adhere to Satan's temptation, who worked through the form of a serpent. Thus his disobedience caused sin to be imputed to all mankind. Note the first two sins were; pride and disobedience. These two are synonymous with all struggles in life abroad.

From this defining moment failure would become the thing we, meaning humans would do best. Sin became synonymous with our character, and great men who would at one point make sincere commitments to God, would be over taken by the lust of their flesh and fall short of their commitment. King David the king of the Jews, chosen by God himself, because of lust disregarded his loyalty to God and committed adultery with a woman named Bathsheba, who was the wife of his loyal servant and lead warrior Uriah. Because David also impregnated her, he could not stop there. He continued his plummet by secretly murdering Uriah to avoid any further controversy. As we can see there is a process in making decisions; first a thought, then a choice, then a action. **A thought** is to conjure up a scenario conceived from experience or desire. **A choice** is to have the option to choose between at least two different things. But the decision comes upon you taking **action,** which is to carryout thought and choice. Time has proven that these three things can alter the outcome of ones existence. It is not true to say that we were created to fail, but were created to choose. Adam could have chosen everlasting harmony with God, but instead he "gambled with destiny." It is true that because of one man's disobedience all were made subject to sin. But it is also true that because of one man's sacrifice, and obedience, that all are given life eternal again, and the capability through the

11

Spirit of God to never fall. Lazily the body of Christ has exaggerated, and misinterpreted the Word of God and referred to passage's that at face value engages you to think that because of your fleshly nature you must fall. There is no law spiritual or natural that says you must fall. Chances are you will make mistakes because you lack knowledge, but by faith and walking consistently in the Spirit and applying the principles set forth in the Word of God you can walk victoriously, and never fall. It will not be easy, but only "the ways of a transgressor are hard." In the next several chapters you will learn the necessary elements that will keep you from falling.

Chapter I

Faith "The little engine that could"

During World War II there was a major shortage
of gas. The little you may have had, you held on to
it with a tight grip. Smith Wigglesworth was one of
the worlds leading apostles during that era, and was
in his mid 80's. He, by the power of God performed
many miracles in which eyewitnesses have testified
of in recent years. While he was traveling through
Great Britain in dangerous war zones, preaching in
local assemblies he was contacted by a pastor from
a nearby town. The pastor kindly requested that he
come and minister to his church. Apostle
Wigglesworth agreed to come only if the young
pastor would pick him up. Smith Wigglesworth
happened to be in another town several miles away.
The young pastor cared not of what the distance
was. He eagerly made his way and picked up the
Apostle. He arrived safely and promptly with no
hindrances. As they journeyed to their destination in
the 8 horse power engine vehicle, they traveled
through forest terrains which were prime sections of
the war zones. They encountered a set back in the
middle of the night. While in the heart of the forest
and in bomb territory they ran out of gas. They were
miles from their destination with no help in sight.
The young pastor was uneasy and embarrassed
sighting the fact that he was escorting this
prominent man of God whom he invited to minister,
and had now stranded him in a danger zone.
    Apostle Wigglesworth did not panic. He calmly

asked the young pastor "do you have any water?" The pastor said "yes, I keep enough to top off the radiator sir." Apostle Wigglesworth confidently said, "fill the tank with water." The young pastor slightly hesitated thinking what obvious damage this could do to his highly valued vehicle. In those days cars were a rare commodity, and not a dime a dozen. After a moment of lingering in doubt he asserted his faith and acted in obedience to the man of God. The young pastor went and dug out the container of water and proceeded to pour the water into the gas tank. All along Apostle Wigglesworth was praying and believing God for another miracle. It would be no surprise for Apostle Wigglesworth to see water turn into gasoline, because he had seen God raise a dead man through his prayer of faith. The young pastor finished pouring the water into the gas tank and was ready to start the vehicle. He cranked the ignition once and nothing happened, a second time nothing happened, a third time and the engine started and ran smoothly. They went on to their destination with no further hindrances.

***<u>Faith</u> is trusting and believing in something without logical proof...

Our entire existence is based on faith. The question is; who or what is your faith in? More than ninety percent of humans don't have a clue of how electricity works and don't care. But they won't hesitate to flip on a light switch. No one starts a job and gets paid a year in advance. You dutifully get up, go to work, punch the clock all prior to getting paid, and with all hope you expect your paycheck at the end of each pay period. Have you ever awaken in the middle of the night to go to the restroom, and before getting out of the bed you wondered if the floor was still there? Of course not, in all these scenarios you are inadvertently acting by faith.

*CQ (common question): **Why is it when we purposely act in faith to receive things beyond the norm, doubt enters in?** Doubt is the natural reaction or reflex to faith. Doubt is a relative of negativity which is produced by Satan. Doubt must be sent out the moment you believe in order for it to have the best chance at defeating you. This is why before you declare or say something, be sure that you believe it in your heart, and immediately rebuke doubt using the Word of God.

*** All things operate by faith, even God. Hebrews 11:3 says, *"through faith we understand that the worlds have been framed by the word of God."* If God operates through faith we must live by, and operate in faith. If you do not possess faith you will not only fall, but eventually die. Faith is the sustaining force that holds us together and gives us continual hope. 1st Peter 1:5 says, *"we are kept by the power of God through faith unto salvation ready to be revealed in the last time."* * Faith is the lifeline or the very essence of hope.

When it comes to living an absolute victorious life, there is no reason to deem it impossible unless you don't believe you can. Faith begins the moment you believe, and the moment you believe will be the moment that what you could not see is conceived.

***The Word is activated by faith, and faith by the Word...

The Word is a contractual agreement between God and man. God honors and stand by his Word. The bible clearly conveys that the more the Word of God is registered in you, the more faith you will obtain. Romans 10:17 says, *"so then faith cometh by hearing and hearing by the word of God."* It is simply cause and effect. **What you digest will determine your progress.** The more Word you digest and meditate on, will absolutely cause you to wax strong in your; trust, hope, and belief in God. These three together make up faith. Faith is a weapon that is most effective when used through the Word. When Jesus had fasted forty days and nights he was then tempted by Satan. He immediately combated his tempter with the Word of God. *So we overcome temptation and all things by faith through the Word of God

***Satan does not want you walk by faith, because then you become invincible!

You must know that you can live in absolute victory over sin. Matthew 19:26 says, *"Jesus beheld them and said with men this is impossible but with God all things are possible."* Man has taken on limitless faith in the natural, believing he can do virtually anything. Man believed that the earth was round, so he stepped out and proved it. Man believed he could fly, and he did it. He believed he could walk on the moon, he did that too. Amazing the things we can do when we believe they can be done. The astronomical things that we do in the natural, we can do even more in the Spirit. When you decide to apply your faith to walk upright before the Almighty God, you will accomplish it. There's no law that says you have to fall. You can consistently walk upright by: *"walking by faith and not by sight"*, (2nd Corinthians 5:7) also *"walking in the Spirit and not fulfilling the lust of the flesh"* (Galatians 5:16).

***Consistency breeds success…

Notice the employee that can work at the same job for 30 years and not quit. We can have that same kind of spiritual stability. Colossians 2:5 says, *"for though I be absent in the flesh yet I am with you in spirit joyfully beholding your order and steadfastness of your faith."* Paul was excited because, even though he was not there preaching to them night in, and night out. They remained strong in their faith concerning Christ. The pastor preaching on Sunday and teaching on Wednesday should not be the sole reason you are maintaining your faith in God. We must excel to the point in our walk that we can grow even in the wilderness and not be over taken. Psalms 119:11 says, *"thy word have I hid in my heart that I might not sin against thee."* Of course we need leadership, but we also must have faith to sustain while not under the direct supervision of man.

***Stick and build upon your faith daily!

Your faith in God must become so strong that you are willing to die for Christ sake instead of living for Satan. 1st Timothy 4:1 says, *"now the spirit speaks expressly, that in latter times some shall depart from the faith giving heed to seducing spirits and doctrines of devils."* People are straying from the body of Christ in large numbers clinging to denominations and doctrines that don't teach holy living. They search for a place that will teach something to better fit their way of living. The bible says in Ephesians 4:5 *"one Lord, one faith, one baptism."* The one Lord is Jesus Christ. The one faith is believing in Jesus Christ, and what Jesus taught the apostles. The one baptism is the baptism of the Holy Spirit with fire, but not denying water which is a symbolism of the burial, and resurrection of Jesus. There is no two ways to God, but only one way, by having firm faith in Jesus Christ. Remember, a *"double minded man is unstable in all his ways"* James 1:8. *Build upon what you know to be true in your heart, not what you want to be true in your mind.

***Do not let your faith waiver because of your circumstances...

Where there is doubt faith cannot exist. 1st Corinthians 2:5 says, *"that your faith should not stand in the wisdom of men but in the power of God."* My first experience exercising faith in the supernatural came in my late teens. Me, and a brother in the Lord were walking under the anointing believing God could do anything. We were yet to have an opportunity to exercise our faith in a church setting up to that point, until one night after a revival service. We decided to tarry behind and worship in the sanctuary. When the time came for us to leave we made our way down the aisle where we encountered a lady who was known to be very sickly with a disease we knew not of. Upon our greeting her she abruptly passed out at our feet. Her name was Rose. Rose stood about 5 feet tall and weighed a mere 85 or 90 pounds. By traditional policy in the church we attended, we were not allowed to lay hands because of our age being so young. The Holy Spirit told me simply to speak in her ear and say, "Rose get up in Jesus name." We did it without hesitation, and she immediately opened her eyes, got up, and worshiped. The amazing part in recollection is, we didn't check for a pulse. For all we knew she could have been dead. Point being, if we had known or thought she was dead we may have doubted because of something so severe and God's work would not have been accomplished. *When God speaks clearly to your spirit don't linger in doubt, just obey. Romans 4:20 says, *"He (Abraham) staggered not at the promise of God through unbelief: but was strong in faith, giving glory to God."*

***What would Jesus do?

Jesus clearly instructed us where our faith should rely. Mark 11:22-24 says, *"and Jesus answered them saying. **Have faith in God.** For verily I say unto you that whosoever shall say unto this mountain be thou removed and be cast into the sea and shall **not doubt** in his heart but shall believe those things which he says shall come to pass he shall have whatsoever he says. Therefore I say unto you what things you desire when you pray believe that you have them and you shall."* An important key, or the very key reason we fall is because our faith is in the wrong source. These three verses summates faith, and shows what can happen when faith is put in God. First have faith in God, not man or your own ability. Know that God can do anything if you believe, and not doubt. This is the first step to not falling. *Have faith for spiritual steadfastness moreover than any other request.

***When you can't see it, you can have it!!!

Faith is not what you can see, it is what you cannot see. Hebrews 11:1 says, *"now faith is the substance of things hoped for and the evidence of things **not seen**."* Many people spend their time praying for things they can easily obtain through natural means and abilities they already possess. When you don't know how to get what you want, that's when God wants to give it to you. God is sovereign, and He is defined by His ability to not be comprehended. The things that are visible were first invisible then spoken into manifestation by the Word of God the Father. God is invisible to the natural eye just as He was in the Old Testament, aside from rare supernatural occurrences. God became visible through Jesus in the New Testament for a specific purpose in time. Jesus said in John 14:9 *"he that hath seen Me hath seen the Father."* God has returned to, and remains invisible for the distinct reason that your faith will not be established in figurines or what you can see with your fleshly eyes. This unique paradigm has been established in order for you to continue to walk by faith in the Holy Spirit, which is the only way you will be able to see God. God cannot be belittled to be seen by the filthy eyes of our flesh. He is too sacred and most holy. When you can't see how you will make it through be encouraged, because that's when God is in control.

***To please God is to believe God...

How many believers pray to have a Spirit filled life like Enoch or Elijah, who were so pleasing to God that they did not see death? They would not have been able to accomplish such a consistent and dedicated life to God without faith. Hebrews 11:6 says, *"but without faith it is impossible to please Him."* There is nothing wrong with desiring to be spiritually great, this should be your greatest desire.

It is a definite truth that faith pleases God. Faith is the root of all creation. You are a direct result of faith, and you can operate in faith to cause things that don't exist, to exist. The same way you were spoken into life by God your father; is the same way you who are in the image and likeness of God can speak the Word by faith, and see manifested results. Each time you make a literal act of faith, God receives pleasure through it. *God is pleased simply because you believe.

***Just do it by faith

You were given dominion over all the earth and its habitat the moment you became a believer and follower of Christ. You were transferred into the Kingdom of Heaven, and the King who is our God in heaven made it clear to us that if we ask for anything by faith in Jesus name, and will not doubt we will receive it. I know it's easier said than done, but **you must say it, believe it, and receive it**. The benefits of being a faith filled believer is, the work has already been done for you to receive the promises of God. The things we desire here on earth to glamorize our life are things we deserve. 2nd

Corinthians 8:9 says, *"Jesus Christ though he was rich, yet for your sakes he became poor that ye through his poverty might be rich."* Children of the Most High God should be wealthy, and the rulers of the wealth of this wicked world. Proverbs 13:22 says, *"the wealth of the sinner is laid up for the righteous."* It is only when you rest your faith in natural things and become dependant on your own abilities, this is when you fall. Faith is the first step, because you must first believe in God, to walk with God. It is by faith that you will accomplish total victory, and by mastering all the steps recorded in the following chapters. Let your faith carry you on!

Chapter II

Diligence "The breakfast club"

Imagine being one of the biggest sports icons in the history of the television era, and carrying the constant pressure to perform each night at the highest level and succeeding at it. Obtaining wealth beyond your dreams, while being respected as a hero. It is a true story for one man from a small town in the south. His quest for greatness and perfection as a basketball player would begin in the early years of his life. Upon entering high school he felt he was good enough to make the team right away with no problem. He tried out for the varsity team in his sophomore year and was cut. Disappointed but determined to make basketball his destiny, he used his disappointment for fuel to work harder than ever during the upcoming summer to insure he would make the team in his junior year. He worked on his game endlessly waking at dawn shooting hundreds of jump shots each day, and exercising his body to its extreme. He tuned his mind in totally on reaching his goal. His hard work paid off and he made the team in his junior year, and went on to be a high school phenomenon. He was recruited by one of the top NCAA division one schools in the nation. Where he continued his excellent play and led his team to a national title. He was sought after highly by professional scouts. He entered the NBA draft and was selected in the first round. He took the league by storm. Scoring at will and flying to heights that fans had never seen before. He had a style and swagger that captured the sports world. The sport became second nature to him. He was the best athlete on the planet at the time.

He remained determined to be the best player year in and year out, and wanted to be considered the greatest of all time. Still young in the league he escalated his pursuit by starting his own workout sessions with some of the players on his team. The workouts would be in addition to the team workouts, and was called, the "breakfast club." It consisted of 6 a.m. grueling workouts and restricted diets. Some of the guys thought he was a maniac, but instead he was merely driven for perfection. Here's a guy on top of the world with riches, respect, power, and clearly the best at his profession. But he noticed that throughout history the great ones never stopped striving to become better. The historic greats would become disappointed if they had one small mishap in their craft. He cared not what anyone else thought of him. He wanted to set the bar high, and he did just that. No one has reached it as of yet. By the end of his career he tallied up several championships, multiple most valuable player awards, record setting performances, and he remained at the top of the NBA each year he played. He believed "you could be born good, but greatness would have to be earned." His success was enormous simply because of his persistent and continual work ethics which is the definition of diligence.

***<u>Diligence</u> is a persistent, consistent, and sincere working effort in doing something...

It would be astronomical if a mere thirty percent of the body of Christ had the same determination, and dedication for spiritual greatness as the previous mentioned athlete did toward a mere leather ball and metal rim. Why is it that believers refuse to make a dedicated effort to walk pleasing before the Creator? Is it because we cannot see our eternal reward with our natural eyes? Instead of being diligent we have become a lazy and methodical generation. We are only diligent from a pious stand point. We go to church out of routine and negate our daily relationship with the Father. The problem is not with the church you attend or your pastor; but it is when you are not in constant connection with God, and seeking Him **only** on a Sunday to Sunday basis. This sort of action starves your spirit man, inevitably causing you to die.

***It pay$ to seek God...

Hebrews 11:6 says, *"He is a rewarder of them that **diligently** seek him."* If a man can love a game such as the previous character we read about, to the extreme that he can dedicate his self to shooting hundreds of jump shots a day. Why can't professing believers pray two or three times a day, and read the Word of God every day. It doesn't have to be a long prayer it just has to be sincere and consistent. It is not how much Word you read, it is how much you understand.

Ask the Father for a deeper understanding of His ways. Seek out His wisdom, instead of the wisdom of this world. The wisdom of this world is the ways of Satan. Do not seek after non eternal things. Seek and trust in eternal things. Colossian 3:1 says, *"if ye then be risen with Christ seek those things which are above where Christ sits at the right hand of God."* It is a good thing to work hard and use your God given talents and abilities to obtain the more exclusive things in this life, but your true treasure is in heaven. Heaven is what you are supposed to be striving for. Colossians 3:2 says, *"set your affection on things above not on things on the earth."* The rewards of this present world are temporal and corruptible. The rewards of diligently seeking after the will and ways of God are incorruptible and never ending in pleasure. God reacts to what you desire, and what you desire is what you will acquire. He does not act outside your will that would defeat the purpose of your unique creative design to be a free will person. God only gets pleasure when you consciously choose Him. When you choose God, you choose success. God is like a spiritual bank the more you put in, the more you get out plus some.

***Preparation results into a consistent lifestyle…

When I enlisted in the U.S. military the first thing that I had to do before I could begin active duty in the field was attend boot camp. There I would be prepared physically and mentally to help prevent me from unnecessary failure. Boot camp was the determining ground that would prove my desire to succeed as a soldier. You must be prepared in order to prevent costly mistakes. Remember the five P's; "PROPER PREPARATION PREVENTS POOR

PERFORMANCE." In Ephesians chapter six Paul describes specific battle gear we must dawn for the daily battle we face. The gear described in chapter six verses 11-18 were designed distinctively for the believer's initial daily survival. The first fruits of your day belong to God, rather it be in; song, prayer, reading the Word, or any form of Godly worship. Ask yourself this question, do I have a consistent daily devotion with God, or am I just a sporadic periodic worshiper? Develop a routine or agenda that causes you to perpetually seek God throughout the day. I have no knowledge of a job where the employer says "oh just come in when you want and I'll pay you." Your employer gives you a set schedule and you make sure that you follow it. There is nothing wrong with you setting devotion times, and holding yourself accountable to those times. True believer's must make constant pursuits of excellence, and a diligent effort towards holiness. **The battle you are in was rigged for you to win! *CQ: why is it that when I set out to seek God in prayer, reading, fasting, or worship I become physically tired?** This is called the spirit of heaviness and a common reaction and response from Satan, along with your flesh in order to keep you from connecting with the Father. This development further proves that what you desire to do in reference to seeking God is beneficial, and also is what you should be doing. Isn't it funny how you never get too tired to eat, or watch television, or play a game? There is no good in the flesh. The flesh does not want to see you become one with the Spirit. It is your personal responsibility to take dominion over the spirit of heaviness and put on a garment of praise by declaring strength in Jesus through the Word of God which clearly states in 2nd Corinthians 12:9 *"My strength is made perfect in weakness."* Isaiah 61:3 says, *"He'll give you the garment of praise for the spirit of heaviness."* The Word gives life, and life equals strength, so you can use the Word to come against all odds.

***Our lives must become engulfed with seeking God…

Paul wasn't joking nor exaggerating when he said in 1st Thessalonians 5:17 *"pray without ceasing."* That does not mean pray 24/7, or spend the rest of your life on your knees. But even when you can't get on your knees, be yet praying in your heart. For instance, when you're in a business meeting or at a birthday party, prayer should always be probing the perimeters of your mind. Prayer keeps you in tune with the Spirit and is the number one form of seeking God. David said, *"one thing have I desired of the Lord, that I will seek after; that I may dwell in the house of the Lord forever"* Psalms 27:4. This is the attitude that all believers must develop. You must acquire an obsession for the presence of the Almighty. There have been many times in the past that I lost my zealous desire for God, but each time I simply asked for God to restore my passion for Him, and He did.

***Your diligent walk and pursuit of God will take you to limitless places.

We should strive to have the same close walk with God as our fore fathers did. Genesis 5:24 says, *"Enoch walked with God and was not."* Imagine walking so close with God, until God finds death unworthy to take you. 2nd Kings 2:11 says, *"Elijah went up by whirlwind into heaven."* Many will say that this is not logical thinking, to be like these gladiators of the faith. But by all means we should strive after perfection. The bible says in Psalms 37:37 *"mark the perfect man and behold the upright for the end of that man is peace."* Why stop at second best when God has designed for you to experience the very best. Don't put limitations on your success, because God surely hasn't. God desires for you for you to grow insurmountably. In most cases we have cut off our own progression in life because we stop seeking the imminent will of God.

*** Never stop pursuing!

Paul said in Philippians 3:14 *"I press toward the mark for the high calling of God in Christ Jesus."* Many of us come to points of satisfaction in our walk with Jesus. We put limits on our spiritual growth. There is no limit of growth in Christ. Just when you think you have arrived, then you must continue to press. How can you conquer something you cannot fully comprehend? The profundity of God cannot be conceived by mortality. As long as you are alive and until the day of Christ triumphant return you will be a mortal. On the other hand, you also have the Spirit of God, and must practice existing and growing in Him. Your flesh only desires to breed immorality. But the Spirit of God that is freely given breeds abundant life. Contrary wise, Satan working through the flesh will never stop pursuing your soul, so should you never stop pursuing God, who by His Spirit will cause you to overcome Satan.

***Purpose is never ending!

You may have fulfilled one area of God's plan for your life, but that doesn't mean you take a vacation from seeking God. This is when you ask the Lord, what is the next big thing you have for me to do? We go from glory to glory, and faith to faith. **God is endless. Our purpose is endless, and our destiny is eternal.** Until you reach heaven there remains a purpose for you to fulfill. The next thing God leads you to do maybe totally different from the previous things God instructed you to do. Your job is to stay positioned to be used effectively by God. *You are only effective when you are connected.

***Have passion, and fear for Christ...

A very key reason you will find yourself on a roller coaster going up and down round and round is; you haven't really developed a true passion for what you believe. More frankly put you really don't care. A definition for passion is a compelling emotion, and devotion to something. True positive passion drives you towards the thing you believe in. Passion is a result of relationship, and relationship is a result of constant communication. As you constantly communicate with God through prayer, His Word, and simply confessing your faults, you will notice a relationship developing quickly. It is your consistent effort to live a holy lifestyle that will result in a relationship that God honors. When you purposely commit sin you immediately sever your relationship with the Father. Remember, in any meaningful relationship there will dwell passion.

Many do not care the way they say they care, or they would be doing what they said they would do. One minute they love God, and the next minute they are caught up in sin profusely. This is a result of a person who does not fear God. If you do not fear God you will never succeed and cannot say that you respect His authority. Fearing God is simply a revere and respect for who He is, and what you know He requires from you. Ecclesiastes 12:13 says *"fear God and keep his commandments for this is the whole duty of man."*

*CQ: Why can't I clearly hear from God? Many wonder why they don't hear from God. John 10:27 says, *"My sheep hear my voice and I know them, and they follow me."* The key word in that passage is "my" showing ownership. Every child identifies with their parents voice simply because they have spent time with them day and night year after year. The more time you spend seeking after God, you become a child that can hear, and be heard. Your level of diligent pursuit results in recognition by God. Remember God is not like you and me, so He will not always speak the way you think, or want Him to with an audible voice. Many times He speaks in unique manifestations such as: signs, dreams, visions, and confirmation through other people.

***The natural cannot produce the spiritual, but the spiritual can produce the natural...

Notice Jesus was conceived by the Holy Spirit, but born through the natural. The key to good success is, don't seek after the things of this world, but seek the Kingdom of Heaven. If you want to see immediate results in the natural you must initiate a quest for righteousness. Avoid being one of the one's who sit and wait for God to find them, God has already found you. In some cases it may be hard to see Him, primarily because your circumstances have blinded you with hopelessness. But learn to see through the eyes of the Word, which shows the true plan and promises of God clearly. I am a witness that there is no hope without Jesus Christ. I tried everything according to my natural power and intellect, and I failed miserably. My success began when I made a concerted effort to live in cohesion with the Spirit of God. As you learn to live in the Spirit of God, great things will manifest out of you.

***The more you are in His presence, the less you are in carnality...

Galatians 5:16 says, *"Walk in the Spirit and you shall not fulfill the lust of the flesh."* A diligent effort to walk in the Spirit will prevent you from falling. The flesh is related to anything non spiritual. I personally found myself engulfed in watching sports to the point that I was negating quality time with the Lord. I felt that because sports are supposed to be clean entertainment, then I could watch as much as I wanted to. But sports and many other hobbies are good in there respective places, but they are not beneficial to your spiritual growth. Never find yourself to be more diligent in carnal pleasures, more than your spiritual pursuit of excellence. In case you missed something, be diligent in these; prayer, worship, the Word of God, and having a consecrated mind. It is Satan's desire to stop you the moment you find momentum, but remember your purpose and go after it with the power of the Holy Spirit.

Chapter III

Virtue "The real 40 year old virgin"

The life of a professional athlete beholds numerous temptations. Their lifestyle is one that is extremely profiled. It is filled with money, exotic women, expensive hotels, fancy cars, top security and some. The ratio of non believers in Jesus to believers is about ninety nine to one. The atmosphere would seem nearly non survivable for anyone trying to live a devoted life for Christ. But if you were a person who possessed the God given talent to play sports and had the opportunity to get paid millions of dollars for doing it, chances are you would. In return if you are a follower of Christ, it is a misfortune that you will have invited in temptation beyond the norm. For one Christ believing NBA player it was a challenge he was willing to take, and was determined to remain pure while doing it. D.C. Brenan grew up with a passion for two things, God and basketball. But he refused to let basketball separate him from God. He entered the NBA in the mid eighties. D.C. was in his early twenties and a true and disciplined believer in Jesus Christ. Impressively he was still a virgin. D. C. took great pride in his Godly beliefs and refused to give into the constant temptations. He stood in the face of temptation every night for a 17 year NBA career. His teammates pressured him to compromise his lifestyle many times over. Many of his teammates would set him up with extravagant women expecting him to give in, but Mr. Brenan held his ground sternly. To make things even more appealing D.C. Brenan spent most of his NBA career in one of the most glamorous cities in the world. A city that is known for its high profiled anything goes lifestyle, Los Angeles California. Brenan won multiple championships over the stint of his career. As his basketball fame continued to escalate, so did the fact that he was a proud virgin that was well pass the common age. The more the media learned of his devoted lifestyle, the more he was exposed as a somewhat strange type of guy. It was hard for the public to believe that Brenan had remained a virgin year in and year out, and had no immediate plans for marriage. But Brenan was a God fearing man that would not just take on a wife to fulfill his physical needs, and risk destroying a legacy in which took him many years of diligent toil and commitment to build. He knew he had to wait on God's best. The best would be the woman God had specifically designed for him. I'm sure he may have preferred to be married much earlier in his career, but that wasn't God's plan, and God's plan was what he was determined to follow. D. C. Brenan completed an impressive NBA career where he played for such teams as; the LA Lakers, Phoenix Suns, Dallas Mavericks, and the Miami Heat, and tallied up a still standing record of 1,110 consecutive games played. Atop of all the millions Brenan had earned, and all the championships he won, none of that compares to the gallant feat he accomplished of remaining pure before God his entire career. D.C. Brenan's life is an inspiration, and an example of virtue. Not long after Brenan finished his perennial basketball career, God sent him a beautiful wife.

***Virtue is the act of being morally good, pure or making the right decisions...

Life is full of constant temptation and will remain. Jesus prayed in Matthew 6:13 *"lead us not into temptation, but deliver us from evil."* When temptation arrives, with it is a growth opportunity. To capitalize on that opportunity you must react in virtue, and not be subdued to the temptation presented to you.

Sin has become more paramount than we have ever imagined, and yet more appealing also. Right and wrong will be two things you will have to choose between for the rest of your existence. But remember without virtue, (or by definition making the right decision), you will not inherit the Kingdom of God. The person that possesses virtue simply does what is morally right. God placed a data base in each child He created. This data base contains all things pertaining to right and wrong. It works like this: the moment you are faced with any scenario, your inner data base, or your brain in accordance with your comprehension level immediately calculates the information and sends a message to your heart, which lets your mind know rather the decision you are making is right or wrong. The data base is called your conscience. 2nd Corinthians 1:12 says, *"For our rejoicing is this, the testimony of our conscience, that in simplicity and godly sincerity, not with fleshly wisdom."* The laws of God were preemptively written in our hearts. 1st John 3:20 says, *"Beloved if our hearts condemn us not than we have confidence toward God."* Your heart will not lead you astray, but your flesh will attempt to draw you into disobedience of what you heart is telling you to do. The heart is the judging platform for God to determine man's intensions. *Your heart always speaks the truth.

***Followers of Jesus must live an exposed life of virtue...

Virtue has gone far from society and the body of Christ must restore it. It seems we can trust no one, but God. The majority of existence has lost all conscience of righteous living and has committed themselves to living in lewdness. The government is blatantly misusing the economic system. The divorce rate has sky rocketed. Abortion is legal and happens more often than the sun rises. Crime is at an all time high and you can find a gun quicker than you can find a penny on the ground. Having children out of wedlock is more popular than getting married and raising a proper family. Homosexuality has become so common they might as well place two men kissing on the dollar bill. Teenage girls refuse to wear any clothes that you don't have to peel off of their body. Sadly, the values of living by a firm rule of ethics such as the bible are no longer being drilled into our youth. Proverbs 22:6 says, *"train up a child in the way he should go and when he is old he will not depart from it."* These are all reasons why believers must take a bold stand for Holy living. We are literally responsible for the future hope of man kind.

***The only wrong way to live is not living for Jesus!

 It is the believer's job to live and exemplary life of holiness seeing that we represent God and His son Jesus. The body of Christ is under a microscope and the world is looking for a reason to ridicule us. We must be living examples at all times. This is all easier said than done.

So you ask how do I obtain virtue? ***You must first develop a hate for sin!*** Matthew 6:24 says, *"No man can serve two masters; either he love one and hate the other."* Your mind must be conformed to holy thinking. A virtuous lifestyle is not something that comes suddenly; but through monitoring your thought process, and quickly rebuking unholy thoughts, you will eventually develop a virtuous lifestyle. Your life should not be a question mark where people cannot identify what you stand for. Your life should clearly reflect Jesus Christ, and His holiness.

*** You are what you think you are!

The decisions you make are a direct result of your thought process. Ephesians 4:23 says, *"and be renewed in the spirit of your mind."* You are not going to just magically become virtuous and remain, but you have to drill yourself daily. The mind must be refreshed into constant moral thinking by the Spirit. Your state of mind is very important to you walking in virtue and sobriety. Philippians 2:5 says, *"let this mind be in you which was also in Christ Jesus."* Having the mind of Christ is to have a mind to do the perfect will of God. The next time you are presented with temptation to do wrong, think of your marriage type commitment to God. Would you commit adultery right in front of your spouse's face? You can hide from man but not from God. Every time we commit an immoral act, we commit adultery towards the Lord. **Defeat always starts in your mind.** Your mind is the place where all your final decisions are manifested. This is the key reason why Satan must attack you here, early and often. You must develop a shield which Paul the apostle refers to as the helmet of salvation. When Satan attacks you with contrary thoughts, reflect and trust in the fact that you are saved by the blood of Jesus Christ, and remember Satan is doomed, and he is aware that he is doomed. Then fight back with the sword of the Spirit which is the Word of God.

***Living virtuously does offer great reward...

What greater reward could Mary the mother of Jesus have received, than to be chosen by God to bare the Savior of the world? Mary was chosen by

God because of her purity. God is a pure and undefiled Spirit and He cannot be integrated among impurity. When you are pure you will produce good things. Living in virtue allows you privileges that many cannot experience. Moreover you will have peace and no guilt, which is a key hindrance to progression towards your destiny.

*** Don't let your past dictate your future!

Be at peace with yourself knowing that your sins are forgiven and that your past is "His-story." The moment you confess and turn from your sins God has taken charge over your past, and has given you charge over your future. 2nd Corinthians 5:17 says, *"If any man be in Christ he is a new creature old things are past away behold **ALL** things become new."* Just because you have a past filled with immoral choices and others around you know of the choices you made, is irrelevant. Every second that goes by is considered the past. Do not allow Satan to hang your past over your head. When he does, hang the Word over his head. It is up to you to determine your future. Will you spend it in depression looking back at your past mistakes, or will you live joyful and exuberant knowing that God has wiped the slate clean. Everyday is a new day in Christ, another chance to live in total victory. Have faith in God that everyday you will walk in holiness believing in Ephesians 1:4 *"According as he has chosen us in Him before the foundation of the world that we should be holy and without blame before him in love."*

***Peace be still!

You cannot obtain peace through any means of your own inventiveness, or any of the world's commonalities. Peace can only be obtained one way, and that is through a constant thought process, focused on Jesus Christ. A lack of peace is what has sent this present society into an inconclusive atrophy. When you have no peace, you have no sanity. When you have no sanity you make wrong immoral decisions. I will state the obvious here; the more you keep your mind on Jesus the more you will make right decision. *When you have peace you have the fullness of God.* Colossians 3:15 says, "Let the peace of God rule in your hearts." You will operate in virtue if you do the following:

Philippians 4:8 says, *"Finally brethren whatsoever things are true, whatsoever things are honest, whatsoever things are just, whatsoever things are pure, whatsoever things are lovely, whatsoever things are of good report; if there be any VIRTUE, if their be any praise think on these things."*

Chapter IV

Knowledge "The atheist"

I met Dan in the latter part of 2005. We worked together in what was a compact and complex environment. Dan was a proud homosexual and active in his atheist beliefs. My first intentions were to stay as far away from him as possible, but the Spirit reminded me that believers should reach out to everyone. Dan displayed a very headstrong persona. He constantly bragged of his past life experiences, his education level, and the prestigious people he was acquainted with. Me, along with my other co-workers all wondered; if Dan's life was so decadent, then why was he working this miserable factory job with us. I had know desire to hold feeble conversation with him. I wanted to get to the real purpose of our encounter. I knew that I was not to establish any form of carnal relationship with Dan. I was aware of my purpose, and it was to challenge atheism head on and minister to Dan. As I engaged in conversation with Dan I hadn't prepared any technical biblical lay out, or studied any historic facts about the Father, or Jesus Christ existence. I was totally dependant on the Spirit and my limited biblical knowledge. Dan knew that I was a believer in Jesus, and seemed to be waiting for me to step forward to defend my belief. Dan possessed vast knowledge and tons of historic facts in regards to why it is not logical that God or Christ do, or ever did exist. That day I noticed the major difference between Christianity and atheism. We have faith, and they think they have facts. I confronted Dan about his atheist practice and asked him to tell me; why is it that he does not believe in God? Dan's argument was, he would rather believe in physical evidence and recorded facts rather than believe in a God that no man has seen, and a mysterious virgin birth. He continued to argue that the bible was nothing but a bunch of mythological stories gathered through the years compiled into a book to help control the behavior of man kind, while acquiring huge financial gain at the same time. He included numerous historic details to back his theory. I was thoroughly impressed by his knowledge. I slowly replied, knowing I was over matched in knowledge. The Holy Spirit led me to ask him the following questions: first I asked, where did you get your facts from? He replied "years of reading and research." My next question was, did you believe what you read? He sarcastically said "obviously." I went on to ask, have you ever met anyone who wrote the literature you researched? He with drawlingly replied, "no." My reply was, "so you got your facts from something you read, written by a person you've never met, or seen with your own eyes?" I noticed the sudden change in Dan's countenance. He realized the simplicity of the thing he had made so complicated. I began to explain to Dan that he had no facts. He had faith just like me. Only his faith is in scientists, and mine in God. His god the scientist with all their knowledge has no conclusion to the big bang theory and no hope of an expected end. Where as my God the Father offers a conclusion and is a God I can feel by His Spirit. Who proves Himself through the fulfillment of His own prophesy and working of miracles. I realized that people feel their knowledge is proven through

51

facts, but ironically their facts are proven through their faith.

***<u>Knowledge</u> is the general awareness or possession of information or facts.

You can have knowledge in several different areas. More importantly is how you exercise what you know, and what areas your knowledge is concentrated in. Your knowledge should be focused on the ways of God first, and everything else second. Mankind has gained knowledge in enormous proportions. Knowledge has been a two way street from the beginning, one being good, and one being evil. From the beginning man chose evil. Till this day man is yet gaining knowledge and using it for corruption. Scientist backed by high powered governmental agencies, continues to create more and more sophisticated explosives and other futile objects. Ecclesiastics 1:18 says, *"for in much wisdom is much grief, and he that increases in knowledge increases in sorrow."* The more you increase in the knowledge of vain non eternal things, only brings more disappointment. The reason being; to have astronomical intelligence of this world and how to advance from a technological standpoint, only benefits you while you are here. This world and all its knowledge, and fancy gadgets shall be destroyed. The only form of knowledge that is never ending and leads to happiness is, to <u>know</u> the perfect will of God.

***When you know God, you know everything!

The first thing you must know and come to terms with is that God is sovereign. You will never fully know the mind and the ways of the Almighty God. It is your duty to make an asserted effort towards knowing as much about God as your mental capacity will allow. Knowledge is progressive only when it is applied properly and used to do well. Just because you know how to kill someone does not mean you should do it. That is a wrongful application of knowledge. Knowledge came in the beginning, in the Garden of Eden. The tree in the Garden of Eden was called the tree of knowledge of good, and evil. This was the tree that God specifically forbid man to partake of. The tree did not obtain any magic potion of sin. The tree simply being there, gave man the power to exercise his unique God like quality to choose. God's desire was for man to choose to obey his inaugural mandate, and remain in everlasting harmony with him. Man after being tempted by Satan in the form of a serpent, chose to disobey. In return he received the curse of sin, and *knowledge* of good and evil. His knowledge would reveal to him many diverse things. Adam was illuminated to the more eccentric wonders of his surroundings, but more notable he learned of the daring evilness of Satan. At one point Adam knew no evil and not many moons after that did Cain, Adam's son murder his own brother Able. Seeing that we have the benefit of knowledge, we must use this unique quality for the glory of God. If you invent something or teach something that causes spiritual or physical decay, it is a sin. 2nd Peter 3:18 says, *"but grow in grace, and in the knowledge of our Lord, and savior Jesus Christ."*

*Learn to measure your success by the knowledge you have of God and His son Jesus.

***Believe what you know…

Your biggest concern must be to consume as much knowledge about God as you can in order to spread His Word properly and effectively. You yourself must first be thoroughly convinced of the validity of Jesus Christ. There should rest no doubt in your mind of who is the only true and living God. If Satan ever challenges you with questions and vain imaginations follow Paul's advice in 2nd Corinthians 10:5 *"casting down imaginations, and every high thing that exalts itself against the knowledge of God, and bringing into captivity every thought to the obedience of Christ."* In the last days as you know there will arise many false prophets that will deceive many. As of right now there are many false doctrines that are stealing away precious souls from the Kingdom of Heaven. 1st Timothy 4:1 says, *"now the Spirit speaks expressly that in the latter times some shall depart from the faith giving heed to seducing spirits, and doctrine of devils."* If you are not equipped with knowledge of the Word for yourself you will fall and be deceived easily by Satan. Stand firm on what you know to be true in your heart.

***The more you know the more you grow!

A baby grows by drinking milk. We grow by our knowledge in the Word of God. 1st Peter 2:2 says, *"as newborn babes desire the sincere milk of the word that you may grow there by."* The most in-depth, and profound book in existence is what we refer to as the bible, but what is the infallible Word of God. What makes this book so prodigious is the fact that it is actually alive. The Word of God continues to manifest itself daily. In light of that fact, you must continue to study the bible in order to receive its habitual release of newly found knowledge. 2nd Timothy 2:15 says, *"Study to show thyself approved unto God a workman that needs not to be ashamed rightly dividing the word of truth."* God's Word shows us how to defeat Satan and how to live in total victory. Many people live beneath their privilege because they just don't know the promises of God and the abundance of His goodness. A primary reason for defeat in any area is lack of knowledge.

***Don't buy fools gold...

The sinner tries to use his or her natural intellect to solve their worries. God through his Word gives us the key to all things pertaining to life. We choose to use the majority of our time and energy focusing on the world systems and their methods of obtaining everything from healing, to financial gain. To think, if the efforts we made to know the mind of God were proportional with the efforts we make to gain more and more worldly knowledge. The astronaut is filled with mathematical and scientific knowledge. Over the past several decades of research, test, and observations NASA has gained the ability to fly deep into the second heaven which is space and explore the planets. They even walked on some these planets. They also have the ability to predict the weather, and set up satellites to monitor the earth. But NASA has no knowledge of how to access the third heaven where God's throne is. The believer in Jesus Christ has the knowledge, and ability through the Word of God, that preponderant geniuses do not possess. 1st Corinthians 1:27 say's, *"but God has chosen the foolish things of the world to confound the wise."* We the body of Christ, know the exact steps necessary to reach Heaven where God almighty dwells. Don't be easily fooled by concepts and genealogies that only pacify your flesh. Believe what you know, and know what you believe. The knowledge of God is an endless quest of learning.

***We should eat so much of the Word, that we become giants crushing sin!

"You are what you eat." Remember that statement, well it's true. It is a sin to glutton natural food, but you can feast off the Word. Proverbs 10:14 says, *"wise men lay up knowledge."* As you obtain vast knowledge of the Word of God it will enhance your spiritual senses causing you to see Satan's devices afar off. **You will not, and cannot know enough about the Word**. Hosea 4:6 says, *"my people are destroyed for lack of knowledge."* The answers to life's most difficult questions are in the knowledge of Christ, and He is waiting for you to dig in deep. Colossians 1:10 says, *"that ye may walk worthy of the Lord unto all pleasing, being fruitful in every good work, and increasing in **knowledge** of God."*

Chapter V

Temperance <small>"In your face"</small>

I was in the 4th grade when my family was forced to live with my dad's mother because of the eviction notice placed on the front door of our house. Dad's side of the family was extremely rambunctious and known for riotous living. My family consisted of; mom, dad, and four siblings, two boys and two girls. I was the eldest of all my siblings by at least six years. The situation we were encountering was new and mind boggling for us. But because of financial reasons we had no choice. To make things even more flustered, two other families were living with grandma already. The house only had two bedrooms so our family totaling six took the sweaty attic. My dad's sister Jeanie and her three children took a room. His youngest sister Pam had two children, and they slept in the living room on the floor and couches. It was grandma's house so she had her own room. The living conditions were meager and embarrassing. The main floor of the house reeked of urine smell so I never invited any of my school pals past the porch. Even though this was the lowest point of our life, and a very discouraging situation we remained faithful to the church, because mother wouldn't have it any other way.

My mother was a God fearing woman and refused to let the worst of situations separate her, or her family from God. Grandma went to church religiously, but no one else in the house ever did.

Aunt Jeanie was a Muslim. Jeanie was very distraught with her living conditions and she showed it with periodic outburst. Whenever my dad was there things remained calm because he showed clear authority. But when he was gone a vindictive spirit would rise up in Aunt Jeanie. She was going through a separation with her husband and didn't want to feel second fiddle to anyone. She saw my family, specifically my mother as some sort of competition. She envied the fact that my mother could find so much peace in a depraved situation. I could tell that Aunt Jeanie's emotions were a balloon ready to burst. Then it happened, it was a normal Sunday morning except dad had to work. Mother prepared us for church as she always did. Aunt Jeanie had an unusual evil spirit that morning, and it would show it's self in rare form. My mother had either left the iron on, or unplugged it prematurely when Jeanie may have wanted to use it next. In any case it was a menial mishap that triggered the unsettled spirit in Aunt Jeanie to erupt. Out of no where she began screaming obscenities directly at my mother. When my mother asked what was it that she may have did wrong, Jeanie in a bull rushing manner charged at her, cornering her in the small greasy kitchen. She continued screaming in a wild banter cursing uncontrollably even threatening to kill her. Spit was flying directly in my mothers face. Mom didn't flinch nor mumble a word. I watched every moment in fear and anger because I couldn't defend mom. My younger brother and baby sisters were crying frantically. Even though I was terrified, at the same time I was amazed at my mother's non retaliation. After Aunt Jeanie noticed that mom wouldn't retaliate, she finally stopped. That's when mom simply said "Jeanie I love you."

Aunt Jeanie broke down in tears, begging for forgiveness.

***<u>Temperance</u> is the act of self restraint in the face of temptation.

This was a prime example of how the devil will attempt to push you over the edge. Notice the devil attacks you the hardest when you are in a vulnerable state. Satan has the power to tempt you, but you have the power to resist him. James 4:7 says, *"Submit yourselves to God, resist the devil and he will flee from you."* To submit means to come under authority. When you come under the authority of God you are under his *"provision, protection, and direction."* Which in turn gives you the ability to overcome all obstacles. God does not tempt us. James 1:13 says, *"Let no man say when he is tempted say I am tempted of God for God cannot be tempted with evil neither tempts he any man."* 1st Peter 5:8 calls the devil your "adversary", which is an opponent. Satan is constantly challenging us to give in to his ways. John 10:10 says, *"The thief comes but to steal, kill, and destroy, but I have come that they might have life, and have it more abundantly."* The devil is wise and knows where, and when to attack you. He sits and waits for an opportunity that he can use to cause you to loose control. Galatians 5:1 says, *"stand fast therefore in the liberty in which Christ has made you free, and be not again entangled with the yoke of bondage."* When you are tempted to compromise or to do evil, quickly do an identity check of yourself and highlight the fact that you are God's child. Satan desires to blind you, and cause you to forget that regardless of the situation you are facing, YOUR VICTORY IS GUARANTEED!!!

***Strengthen your weaknesses, and weaken your strongholds…

It is not wise to place yourself in a position to fall. Superman never went looking for kryptonite because he knew it would destroy him. If you know you are weak in a certain area you must avoid that area particularly, until God builds you up to the point of maturity concerning the situation. Everyone has an area of struggle or weak points. These struggles could have stem from many scenarios such as; generational traits, premature exposure, etc.

In any case you can weaken any strong hold by fasting and declaration of the Word of God. On the flip side you could struggle or be weak in areas that enhance your continual growth in Christ such as; reading the Word, praying, assembling together with believers, witnessing, etc. All these things are vital to your progression.

***Learn to attack the devil before he attacks you...

We defeat the devil in spiritual warfare, not with natural weapons. If you know the areas you lack temperance in you should constantly rebuke those areas in Jesus name, by quoting the Word. Jesus told his disciples to pray *"lead us not into temptation"* (Matthew 6:13), because He knew temptation was coming. Practice having a offensive mind set towards the devil. Attack him early, and often. First identify your weaknesses. Then find scriptural reference and profess your deliverance from that area of temptation. As it was said before and will be said many times after, Jesus overcame Satan with the Word.

***God's word cannot fail!

Remember at what point Satan tempted Jesus, it was after Jesus had fasted. Jesus was physically weak and possibly vulnerable. In His weakest state, still He was able to defeat Satan easily and win effortlessly with the Word of God. When you become weak and cannot fight the situation you are being faced with, do not depend on natural means for fortification. Psalms 105:4 says, *"Seek the Lord and His strength."* You will find strength in the Word, Psalms 119:11 says, *"thy word have I hid in my heart that I might sin against thee."*

***Don't destroy yourself, build yourself!

You should possess temperance in every area of your life. If you are over indulging in anything, it becomes a form of gluttony. Followers of Christ should carry themselves in a modest fashion. Philippians 4:5 says, *"Let your moderation be known to all men."* Moderation means temperate, or mild. Paul in Philippians 2:3 uses the term lowliness of mind, meaning in a humble frame of thinking. America for example has no sense of moderation. This is the key reason we are listed year after year as the number one obese country. Many times we find ourselves eating when we are not hungry. Moreover we are eating badly prepared foods. It is not God's will for you to be obese. In most cases it is gluttony that causes obesity. Gluttony is a sin and a result of no temperance. Many times the first thing you will do when you become stressed is eat, instead of praying. Philippians 3:19 says, *"Whose end is destruction, whose God is their belly, and whose glory is in their shame, who mind earthly things."* These are the ways having no self control can cause detriment. Take pride in knowing that you are a creation of God who has a purpose and deserves a long, healthy, and prosperous life.

***Do not be controlled by your emotions; be controlled by the Spirit...

2nd Timothy 1:7 says, *"For God has not given us the spirit of fear, but of power, love, and self discipline."* In this passage the word fear means cowardice. Of course you should reverently fear God, but you should stand in boldness against Satan and his demons. Don't let Satan play on your emotions causing you to be a tumble weed believer.

As long as you have the Holy Spirit you are in charge. Learning to control your flesh is not easy because the flesh is your primary instinct. Naturally you respond quicker to its desires. Emotionalism can be your ultimate destruction if you do not quickly establish your heart in what you believe. If you only respond to how you feel you will become like the children of Israel going in circles day after day, year after year, and dying in the wilderness. Learn to respond to the Spirit, not the flesh. You can only respond to the Spirit by constantly walking in the Spirit. Peter, Christ disciple was a very emotional person who was quick to draw his sword and respond violently. Jesus told Peter in so many words "if you live by the sword you will die by the sword" Matthew 26:52. Acting on emotions can result catastrophically. It is good to be passionate and contrite, but it is not good when you become a set of emotions controlled by circumstance. Nothing in this world is worth you severing your commitment to Jesus Christ.

***You will always be tempted, but you can always win…

When God created man first came the flesh, then he breathed into them and they became living souls. The spirit is eternal with no depth or height. Because of sin the flesh has an end, and it knows that end is total destruction. Therefore in all envy of the spirit, the flesh influenced by Satan wishes to destroy its self meanwhile destroying the soul as well, which is Satan's ultimate goal. Paul said that he had to beat his body down daily. Meaning, he had to constantly keep his flesh under control. Chances are you will get angry and you will be tempted in small, and large ways. Ephesians 4:26 says, *"Be ye angry and sin not"* Romans 12:21 says, *"do not be overcome with evil, but overcome evil with good."* When temptation comes so does a way to escape. You can conquer, and overcome your flesh, and all the works of Satan through the Word and the Spirit of God the Father.

Chapter VI

Patience "4 minutes in 4 years"

Some dreams never come true, simply because we abort them too soon. Not the case for one high school senior, who dreamed of putting on his high school basketball teams jersey and playing in the game just one time. He was born with what was a rare and little researched disability at the time called autism. His parents didn't notice any irregular symptoms until he was around 5 years old. Autism is a mental debilitating disease, so he was able to operate normal from a physical standpoint. However, he was slow to learn and react. He discovered a passion for sports, particularly basketball at a young age. He refused to let his inabilities stop him from pursuing his dream. When he entered high school he immediately tried out for the basketball team hoping to get a spot even if he didn't play right away. He tried out but was cut, because of his lack of ability to play the game at the high school level. The coach was aware of his disability and admired his enthusiasm. Sympathetically the coach offered him a job as team manager, which is the water boy in reality. He gladly with no complaints accepted the position. He was simply excited about being apart of the team in some intricate way. To his delight he was able to shoot around in practices with the team. In his heart of hearts he awaited the day when the coach would say, "suit up you're playing today." For many moons that never materialized. His senior year arrived and he never heard one iota of the possibility that he would ever play in a game.

He was beloved by the team, and all his classmates. No one cared that he had autism and attended special education classes, they simply loved his spirit. What was a pipe dream was about to become a reality. Little did he know that the coach who had come to love him, decided to surprise him, and the entire community. Can you believe after waiting and serving four years the coach came to him and said; "senior night is coming up, and I want you to suit up. I can't promise you'll get to play, but I will try to get you on the floor." He was blown away and in total awe. This was definitely a pleasant surprise. He didn't care if he played at this point, he just wanted to put on a uniform, and if he played that would be even better. He had played some little league, and played with high school kids in pick up games, but never actually played in an organized high school game. This would be a totally different platform for him. He would be playing with the best his age group had to offer. The best night of his seventeen year old life had arrived. He was nervous and had no clue if he would see any playing time. The news that he would play in the game spread like wildfire. Everyone in the school, and the community knew him, and was excited to see his dream come true. They even made posters and real hand fans with his picture on them. The entire crowd was cheering for him. The night became all about him, and everyone anticipated seeing him get in and take at least one shot at the basket. The atmosphere was that of a NCAA game. The gym was beyond capacity because of him, and no one was sure he would even get in the game. His team would eventually dominate the game leading by 20 points with only 4 minutes to go in the fourth quarter. Knowing he had the game in hand the coach looked down the bench and signaled for him to go in the game. As he walked to the scorers table to check in, the crowd was already in a loud banter, and at that point they became three times louder. This is the moment they waited for. He checked in the game. His team was on defense and after a turnover his team got the ball up by 20 points, they were only concerned about letting him score. They immediately passed him the ball, he was wide open for three and he shot it clear over the rim. It was an air ball. The crowd let out a huge awe! His team got the ball again and now there was only 3:12 left in the game. Again he was open, this time he nailed the shot, nothing but net. His team got another rebound off a missed shot. They passed him the ball at the other end, and with a hand in his face amazingly he hit another three point shot. The crowd was in a frenzy! With only 90 seconds remaining, he supernaturally hit three pointer after three pointer scoring 20 points in just 4 minutes on the floor. The entire gymnasium was in absolute pandemonium. No one could believe what had just taken place. He was carried off the floor like a hero. This young mans patience paid off in astronomical form.

***<u>Patience</u> is the ability to endure waiting, without becoming annoyed or upset when faced with difficulty.

Was the microwave invented for our convenience? No, it was because heating up food the old fashion safe way became just to slow in our fast paced world. Nearly everything has evolved from a moderate timely process, to instant gratification. Everyone seems to be in a rush to go nowhere fast. In all logic, why would we create a vehicle that tops out at a speed of 160 miles per hour when the speed limit is no more than 70 miles per hour? Today's society is moving at such a frantically fast pace, we are bound to crash someday. I became so spoiled with high speed internet, until I wouldn't even check my email at a computer that didn't have high speed internet. By all means the convenience and ability to do things fast is well appreciated, but it makes you accustomed to not being willing to wait. We must realize that time was implemented for a purpose. Time was not created for God, because God is infinite and cannot be subjected to time. Time was created for man to go through the process of evolving into perfect completion. In every age and facet of existence, time has told the true story. Realize that you don't control time, but you can dictate what happens in time.

***Waiting yields great rewards. "When wait you become great"!

David was anointed as king of Israel as a young teen, suspected around fifteen years old. He waited and served Saul his present king at the time faithfully. He even fought and won battles for him. David knew that he was the anointed king, but he did not rush his calling whatsoever. David accepted the fact that it was not his time to be king, and made his self content with his current position. Ironically patience is developed over time. James 1:4 says, *"let patience have her perfect work in you that ye maybe perfect entirely wanting nothing."* Patience and time are siblings. Time allows you space to develop patience, and developing patience makes you perfect. One of my favorite verses 1st Peter 5:10 says, *"but the God of all grace who hath called us unto his eternal glory by Christ Jesus after that ye have suffered A WHILE, make you perfect, establish, strengthen, and settle you."*

***God does not accept mediocrity...

Always remember that you were made in the image of the perfect one. Of course you are burdened with the flesh and its lust, but you also have many resources to combat your flesh. It is your job to use every outlet of defense in order to walk in total victory. To whom much is given, much is required. Many times **you are challenged with a lot because you are destined to accomplish a lot**. Matthew 5:48 says, *"Be ye perfect as your Father in heaven is perfect."* As previously stated, perfection is a result of patience, and patience is an element of waiting, and waiting is an element of time. Sometimes in life you experience long periods of void space and it seems nothing is happening. When you are in this state continue to build upon the purpose that God has revealed for your life, by prayerfully "writing the vision and making it plain." Instead of doing nothing, do something progressive toward the dream in your heart. For God to multiply or even recognize your desire you must act in faith toward it. "Faith without works is dead" so says the book of James. When you have been patiently waiting and preparing, God will come along and give you increase, and the manifestation of your desires.

***As you wait you elevate!

As you exercise your ability to wait in contentment you develop patience. As your level of patience continues to heighten, you will eventually gain full maturity in your walk. When we become hasty and anxious we tend to move out of season. You don't plant tomatoes one day and expect to pluck them the day after. 1st Corinthians 3:6 says, *"I have planted, Apollos watered; but God gave the increase."* When you move out of God's season and timing for your life, you're on your own and you will die prematurely. All things must be released as God allows. You can avoid failure by following God's plan. Ecclesiastics 3:1 says, *"to everything there is a season and a time to every purpose under heaven."* If you become in such a rush to do something chances are you will miss God. Continuing to move under your own direction and your own will, will result dismally. In result when God is ready to release His blessing in your life you will be out of position, and won't receive what God planned to give you. Never think that there is nothing to do in the meantime. Many times you may be so focused on what you want to do until you convince yourself it's the only thing to do. But if you take time to seek God, He will always direct you in what you should be doing while on the road to your destiny.

***Never try to create your own destiny, God already has!!!

Your job is to seek God and wait while in preparation for the fulfillment of His Word. Psalms 37:7 says, *"rest in the Lord wait patiently for him."* This is what you should do while you are waiting on God. The word rest hear doesn't mean do nothing progressive, it means don't worry. When you pray and ask God for something you only need to ask once. Jesus told us not to pray in vain repetitions. Many people will ask God over and over for the same thing year after year. If God says nothing, then the answer is no at that time. Many times God is not saying no, He just isn't saying yes because it is not the right time. Relish His presence, knowing that His Word will accomplish what it was set out to do. Psalms 37:4 says, *"delight yourself in the Lord and he will give you your hearts desire."* If you know God has promised you something rejoice because God cannot lie.

***Don't complain while you wait, praise while you wait!!!

Don't be weary in well doing, encourage yourself in the Lord, embrace time and **"know that your waiting was pre ordained for your perfection to come."**

Realize that patience is something you must have to be successful. You can obtain patience by simply learning the will of God for your life. When you know the will of God you understand His sovereign timing. You know the will of God by seeking Him day and night. When you live in God, and His Spirit in you, life becomes timeless and nothing matters because in His presence is fullness of joy. Isaiah 40:31 says, *"but they that wait on the Lord shall renew their strength, they shall mount up with wings like eagles they shall run and not be weary they shall walk and not faint."*

Chapter VII

Godliness "A woman's quest"

Not long ago there was a woman who purposed in her heart to pursue God like she had never pursued Him before. Her life before the knowledge of Christ was a life that included many diminishing attributes. In spite of her church upbringing, like many she wandered away from the positive spiritual teaching that she had received as a child. As a result her life took many turns for the worst. She came to a point of total hopelessness and despair, and she realized that her only hope of any recovery was surrendering to Jesus. She knew the will of God, but now she was ready to do the will of God. She went through a period of restoration and learning. But in her case the learning curve would be fast because of experience, and the evident anointing that was on her life. This factor played a huge part in her quick development. Knowing the type of person she was, and the type of things she had been exposed to while she was living in sin, she knew that in order for her to maintain a Godly lifestyle she'd have to work extra hard at holy living and perpetuate a consecrated lifestyle. As time went on her desire for Godliness waxed stronger and stronger. She began to desire only one thing and that was the presence of the Lord. Her desire resulted in a rare form of good radicalism. She began pursuing God on plateau's that had never been seen by anyone in her surroundings. God began rewarding her, by elevating her through the leadership that she had faithfully been serving. She took advantage of her position in the local church and began to hold constant all night prayer services. Eventually one full night of seeking God in the sanctuary would not be enough. So she decided to lock her self in the church for seven days and nights. When she wasn't spending the night in the church, she would awake early in the morning and arrive to the sanctuary by five o'clock just to pray and anoint the altar. As a result of a constant, and sometimes exhausting pursuit of God, God continued to reward her immensely. She shot through the ranks and red tape of church politics and evolved into a prominent evangelist. Year by year her fame grew but her passion toward pursuing God never ceased. Her presence was in demand more and more at church gatherings all around the world, and she was prospering enormously. She remained humble and obedient to the voice of the Lord. She came to a point in her life where she was now a national figure specifically in the church sector. She heard the voice of the Lord say "clean the toilets at your local church home." Without question she obeyed. People at the local assembly were in shock and awe that a person of her position and achievement would get on their knees and scrub toilets. She cared not about what people thought, she only wanted to obey God. She realized that she made it to this point in her life because of obedience, and she knew that disobedience would ruin everything. This one woman's quest has yet to stop, and the rewards for her pursuit have yet to stop coming. She still holds regular early morning worship and prayer services, while operating one of the top worldwide ministries.

***<u>Godliness</u> is a devoted life to worshiping God, and having God like qualities.**

Besides going to church how many believers can say they spend at least one collective hour per day in; the Word, prayer, praise, worship, or all. These four things are the only source of accessing, sustaining, and maintaining a Godly lifestyle. We should live a life that is in constant pursuit of more Word, prayer, praise, and worship. There is no designated time to worship. Our life should be engulfed with Gods presence. Psalms 16:11 says, *"in thy presence is fullness of joy."* God is surrounded by joy and purity. Revelation 4:8 says, *"they rest not day nor night saying holy, holy, holy; Lord God Almighty, which was, and is, and is to come."* When you reside in the presence of the Lord you will reap the benefits that surround Him. There is no greater fulfillment than being with God. Every void is filled when you encounter His presence. Depression is not God like. Continual poverty is not like God. Being angry all the time is not like God. So to filter out these negative attributes of the flesh, you must devote more and more time to seeking and dwelling in the presence of your Father.

***Your environment determines your development...

Humans adapt to their environment. For instance if you move to Russia for the next ten years of your life you will be more immune to cold weather, and will also gain a slight Russian accent. This does not mean you are a Russian. Remember you are in the world but not of the world. Don't be a person that adapts to any environment, but rather learn to create and set your environments to a Godly atmosphere. Walk in the authority given to you as a child of the Most High God. You have the power to dictate your surroundings by the power of the Holy Ghost through the Word of God. Godliness is not a two way street, either you're in or out. James 4:8 says, *"draw nigh to God, and he will draw nigh to you. Cleanse your hands ye sinners, and purify your hearts ye doubled minded."* As you separate from sin you will become closer to God.

*** Be changers of the world...

Believers should be in total dominion of the world systems. You are the head and not the tail, above and not beneath. Jesus sacrificed so much for His creation to regain the kingship that was forfeited in the beginning. Many professing believers have decided to compromise. Don't fall prey to society, continue to be peculiar. 2nd Corinthians 6:14 says, *"be ye not unequally yoked with unbelievers for what fellowship has righteousness with unrighteousness, darkness with light."* Stop and think about your circle of friends. Can you think of one person who is worth your eternal life? How will you become like Jesus if you continue to mingle with those who have no desire for Godliness? I never read where God and Satan went out bowling together. You have the power to entertain whatever you want. When you are with, or around the ungodly it is not for you to conform to their ways, but it is an opportunity for you to transform them by being a light. Matthew 5:16 says, *"let your light shine before men that they may see your good works and glorify your Father which is in heaven."* Your environment can cause you to excel or decay. You will always decay if you compromise and conform yourself to the ungodly. You will always excel if you remain not ashamed of Jesus Christ, and focused on walking in His ways.

*** If you can't worship God, you cannot be like God!!!

Worship is the essence of Godliness, and a sign of submission to God. Worship is how we relate to our Father, and how He relates to us. You cannot have a relationship with God if you cannot worship Him. There is only one way you can worship God; as it is stated in John 4:24; says, *"God is a Spirit and they that worship Him must worship Him in Spirit and in truth."* To be in the Spirit you must be flowing with pure intentions, with no ulterior motives. If you are not a true worshipper your lifestyle will reveal it. John 9:31 says, *"now we know God hears not sinners: but if any man be a worshipper of God and doeth His will he hears them."* God responds to true worship because true worship comes from a pure heart. Make a habit of cleansing yourself before worship services. You should always be doing moral and spiritual inventory of your life. You are not required to be perfect in order to worship God, but you are required to be honest. Remember it says "in spirit and in truth." A common statement among the older religious sector was; "I've been saved all week long, and no sin have I done." As to say that this gave them more of a right to worship God than the person next to them who had just gotten saved that day, or the person who was living saved and sinned, but also sincerely repented. Once you've confessed and turned from your sins, you gain access and the right to worship God. The Father is calling for His children to come back to the heart of worship where it's all about Him. The outer court is not where God showed up in the Old Testament, but it was the inner courts where He showed up. Adorning yourself in fine linens and singing exceptionally means nothing if you have not purified your heart. Learn to live from the inside out, because that's all that God sees.

***Be careful that you are not worshiping false gods...

If someone hits your $75,000 luxury vehicle, and you began using profane language and become bellicose, you may be worshiping something other than Jesus Christ. If another believer in the church rightfully corrects your child and you become hostile and angry, you might want to check again who you are worshiping. God comes second to no one, or no thing. We own nothing, it all belongs to God, *"The earth is the Lord's and the fullness there of the world and they that dwell therein"* Psalms 24:1 says. Don't let anything separate you from living a Godly life. God is definitely a jealous God, and you will get more response from Him, when He is first on your list of priorities. The moment you choose anything over God you disconnect yourself from Him. If, or when my wife, mother, children, or siblings die, no matter how they die I will cry immensely, but I will not leave God. I didn't create them, God did. If you are so committed to something that you are willing to sin because of it, you may need to let it go. Where your heart is, will also be where your treasure lies. Be mindful of what Solomon said that "all is vanity", but God. In essence all that matters is the will of God.

***Strive for perfection, don't be just good enough...

1st Timothy 4:7 says, *"exercise yourself unto godliness."* This proves that you must work toward it. Godliness will not evolve over night. I believe you can walk in perfection by constantly walking in awareness and obedience of the Word, and living a life of worship. Peter the disciple of Jesus said "be sober and vigilant." I have obtained this mind set; don't do, say, or think anything that you would not want to be caught up in during Jesus Christ's return. 1st Peter 4:18 says, *"and if the righteous scarcely be saved where shall the sinner and the ungodly appear."* It's either holiness or hell that's what the old church preached, and that's a true saying. Hebrews 12:14 says, *"follow peace with all men and holiness without which no man shall see the Lord."* We must stop trying to "hip hop" Jesus. Many are trying to modernize the gospel and tailor it to fit, and pacify the world. Romans 12:2 says, *"be not conformed to this world but ye transformed by the renewing of your mind that ye may prove what is that good and acceptable will of God."* The sum of the matter is simple; Godliness is to be like

God, not like your favorite superstar. To be like God you must spend quality time with Him, learning His ways and what pleases, and displeases Him. ***You won't live your best life, until you live like God!***

Chapter VIII

Brotherly Kindness

"Granddaddy"

Granddaddy never did things to be seen of men, he did them from his heart. No matter how much he gave or did, he wanted to do more, and wanted no recognition. I cherished taking the twelve hour bus ride as a pre-teen from Detroit to the tiny state of Delaware to be with him in the summer time. After living a less than holy life as a young man, James Timmon gave himself over to a dedicated life of holiness in his mid thirties. As he progressed in his walk with Christ, he knew in his heart he was called to lead and help people. He followed that unction and began shepherding churches in the early eighties where he would eventually birth out several other pastors from that ministry. He was also adamant about feeding and clothing the poor. As I grew older our relationship distance because of the expense of travel, but he was always one phone call away. I can recall a time in my teens when we encountered a hardship in my family that could have torn us apart. Granddaddy became aware of the circumstances and with no hesitation; he drove to Detroit to see about me, my brother, and my two sisters. We were astounded by his quick arrival. He was fully willing in his old age to stay and solve the matter with no regard for time. It was in 1999 when I would be divinely reconnected with granddaddy for and extended period of time. It had been nearly eight years since we had spent quality time together. Granddaddy had moved to the warm state of Texas for his retirement in 1998. Not long after that would he make a sacrifice of love by housing his daughter (my mother), me, and my three siblings. Severe hardship caused us to up root from Detroit entirely, and move to Texas immediately. Granddaddy welcomed us with open arms. By now I was 20 years old. Granddad and I were relating better than ever. He constantly drilled me with the Word of God and the roles and responsibilities of man hood. Our relationship continued to flourish and I gained a reverent respect for him.

My mom eventually moved back to Detroit with my siblings, but I wanted to remained in Texas and spend time with him. I stayed for the next few years learning his ways and mimicking him. He became my spiritual father. I learned that he was a man who refused to say no to a person in need. I witnessed people who borrowed money from him, and never paid him back, and had no intentions to. Nevertheless he treated them the same. That was just one of many scenarios in which others abused his kindness. I was vengeful at their blatant disregard. I wondered, why would he let people take advantage him? I had a Peter attitude ready to draw my sword, and his heart was like Jesus. He told me to never seek refuge against man, just forgive. Granddaddy came to hundreds of people rescue with no desire for reward. He was convinced that his reward was in heaven. He did everything out of brotherly kindness. I indirectly prophesied his death at the beginning of 2003. I said "well granddad you'll be 77 this year, this is the year of completion for you." I did not know he would die later that same year. While he was yet in a coma I went to visit him in the intensive care unit. He began to open his eyes only looking up as toward heaven, and miraculously throwing his hands up in worship as if he saw visions of Jesus. I stood there in total amazement of God's power, and grace upon his life. I knew then that he had his reward, one that no man could give.

***<u>Brotherly kindness</u> is to possess a; sympathetic, compassionate, forgiving, and giving nature.

These attributes are lacking in the body of Christ as a whole. When you see your brother or sister in calamity it is not the time to quote the scripture; "be not deceived God is not mocked whatsoever a man sows that shall he also reap." This is the time you should pray for mercy on their behalf regardless of your personal judgment. Matthew 7:1-2 says, *"judge not that ye be not judged, for with what judgment ye judge ye shall be judged."* Followers of Christ don't laugh, or kick someone when their down, we encourage and comfort them. Galatians 6:1 says, *"brethren if a man be overtaken in fault ye which are spiritual restore such a one in the spirit of meekness*

considering thyself lest thou also be tempted."
Mercy is a key attribute of brotherly kindness. You
can easily develop a merciful outlook by simply
placing yourself in the situation of every person you
meet. Just ask yourself what would I want to happen
to me in this situation?

*** Practicing humility creates stability...

Humility causes you to become drastically closer to
God. Humility forces your flesh to die, and releases
the Spirit of God to have free course. Find ways to
place others before your self. This action
automatically builds humbleness. Believers should
constantly be thinking of ways to bless and help
people, both saved and unsaved, who are less
fortunate than themselves. It would be unwise to
give all you have, but try to give what you can. To
have money and nice earthly possessions is a part of
God's will, but to not be willing to part with some
portion of them, in order to help the less fortunate is
greed, and greed is sin. Giving is what Jesus was all
about, and giving is a paramount form of humility,
and without humility brotherly kindness will not be
displayed. In your quest to be like God your Father

you must develop a heart to give abundantly. The
most popular scripture verse to date is: *"for God so
loved the world that he **gave** his only begotten Son"*
John 3:16. God gave His ultimate sacrifice, His
Son, and Jesus continued giving by giving his very
life. *You can never give enough, but you can give
too little.

***The more you give, will make you one with God...

2nd Corinthians 9:7 says, *"God loves a cheerful
giver."* Of course God loves everyone but he takes
more pleasure in those who are happy about giving.
Your excitement to give shows God that He is more
important than what it is you are sacrificing. The
desire to give comes from God, and it is Satan's
desire to discourage you from giving. You can also
give without giving a physical object or money.
One thing that no one can take away from a person
is time. When you spend quality time with a person
it goes extremely far. When was the last time you
embraced a homeless person? When was the last
time you gave and didn't care about getting back?
You should only expect a return from God, not the

person you gave to. Try to do whatever you can to further a person, and have the satisfaction that you were able to exercise Christ like attributes. This type of mind set guarantees a return. **Man can repay you, but only God can reward you.** These are the behavior traits of a person possessing brotherly kindness.

Practice giving sporadically not just at church. Never give to be seen of men, because man's opinion does not matter. Matthew 6:4 says, *"do your alms in secret and the Father which sees in secret will reward you openly."* *Giving from a pure heart in order to please God, yields immeasurable rewards.

***How many lost souls are you responsible for?

The body of Christ should be a spiritual, and natural bank for the poor and broken hearted all over the world. Disappointingly only a small percentage of the body of Christ is supporting the furtherance of the gospel. You can support the work of Christ in many ways, especially in day to day outreach, reaching out to people you see in desperate situations. Would you be willing to take your two week vacation and spend it in a third world country volunteering? There are thousands of people who should remove the title missionary and minister from their name. Missionaries and ministers were not designed to speak for ten minutes on Friday and Sunday nights. But they are to serve in their communities and all nations faithfully. Ephesians 4"1 says, *"walk worthy of the vocation wherewith ye are called."* Don't say you're called, and then go hide in a box. You don't have to travel the world, but you must seek the will of God outside of the four walls of the church. How many people can be reached in a 300 hundred seat sanctuary? This is the reason Jesus traveled so much. Jesus wanted to reach as many as He possibly could in a three year period. Maybe you are not able to travel with the gospel, but try and support the many diverse ministries who have committed their lives to taking the gospel to the world. Every time you consider someone else, you are acting in brotherly kindness.

Believers in Christ must now more than ever display the livelihood of Christ, putting personal agendas aside and putting the needs of mankind first. Sitting in pulpits will get you know where if you are not preaching and helping people everywhere. God has called the body of Christ to be a lender and a witness to all the nations. This mandate can only be fulfilled by the unification of all believers.

***One church!!!

Man made denominations has only caused the body of Christ to divide. The word denomination is not in the Word of God. But the word doctrine is, and there is only one doctrine that should be taught, and that is the doctrine of Jesus Christ. John 7:16-17 says, *"my doctrine is not mine, but His that sent me. If any man will do His will, he shall know of the doctrine, whether it be of God, or whether I speak of myself.* As of 2007 there are 33,800 different denominations on record. This is a very apparent trick of the enemy. We will not win the world until we unite in the name of Jesus Christ. Ten churches with ten people and ten separate set of expenses, would do better if they were to unite as one; making one church with one hundred people and one set of expenses. The process is simple. It is the humility part that is hard for man to do. Check yourself to be sure that you don't possess the spirit of competition, but instead the spirit of completion. We are here to complete and benefit one another. Our fight is with Satan, not each other. For what reason should I fight against a team member. We should be busy working towards being a cohesive spiritual unit with one purpose, to serve God through Jesus, by the Spirit together.

***Don't let yourself get in the way...

Jealousy and selfishness has taken the place of brotherly kindness. No one has time to stop by the wayside and minister to that destitute person anymore. We have become way to busy for the things that actually define the word ministry. Pride always comes before a fall, and you always see pride coming. You can avoid pride by always identifying your purpose for creation: which is to please God and be with Him, not to try and be God. Paul the apostle counted all that he had accomplished as a lost for Christ sake. He realized that his purpose for living was to please God. He pleased God by giving of himself for the benefit of the kingdom. The kingdom is benefited only when souls are stolen from Satan's hand. We draw sinners with kindness and love. Jeremiah 31:3 says, *"with loving kindness have I drawn thee."* How can mean spirited people draw someone to Christ? How can a jealous and envious person proclaim that they are a believer in Jesus? Matthew 7:6 says, *"ye shall know them by their fruits."* Do not let your life become one big competition with other people. We are all joint heirs in the Kingdom of God. We all have the same rights. It is not about being, having, or building the biggest thing. But it is about being as effective as you possibly can for the sake of the kingdom. Why be jealous or envious of your brother when they prosper, instead rejoice with them. Jealousy and envy will lead to tragedy, just as it did with Cain killing his brother Able in the book of Genesis. These two negative ways have split many nations, families, friendships, and fellowships. Romans 12:10 says, *"be kindly affectionate to one another with brotherly love in honor preferring one another."* Notice the latter of the verse preferring one another. Always look to do for someone else. Constantly rebuke your fleshly pride, and self centeredness. If your brother or sister is in a bad situation pray for them, and give them words of encouragement, and embrace them. These moments come in life for you to express the likeness of Jesus, not to turn against your brother or sister.

Chapter IX

Love "A true Love story"

"My Son, hear me and understand. Our creation has rebelled against us. Their immorality has multiplied greater and greater day by day. They take no reverence in their creator. They despise all that is good, and honor all that is evil. They rather create false gods made of hands than worship me the true and living God. I have shown them my wondrous works over and over, and yet they choose to deny my power and choose to fulfill their flesh. Sin has piled up among them as heaps of coal. They religiously offer burnt offerings that now pierce my nostrils with foul odor. I have given myself but two options. The first being: I destroy what has become an abominable creation, and the second I give to them a Savior that is perfect in everyway. A Savior that has no ability to sin, but can feel their burden of sin. A Savior so pure, if he sacrifices his life he will redeem, and reconcile this reckless people unto me, and I will forgive them of all their sins. My Son as I have searched all the heavens and all the earth none of my creation, not even the chief of my angels come close to you, for you and I are one. You are perfect, and shall always remain perfect. I am your Father and this I ask of you, to be my ultimate sacrifice. I will remove you from glory and cloche you with a sinful body. You shall do no sin, but you shall feel sins misery, and temptation. You shall not be received as a king, but as one who blasphemes. You shall be hated because of your good works. The leaders of the land along with your own kindred will seek to murder you by form of crucifixion. One of your trusted followers will betray you and give you into the hands of your accusers. You will be taken in front of the leaders and suffer false accusation, but you will not defend yourself. Your own people will lobby that you be crucified with no reasoning. They won't just crucify you; first they will mock you, and spit upon you, and strike you with their hands. They will place a crown of 72 thorns upon your head. This is only the beginning of your painful suffering. They will bind you up and find the worst of objects to beat you all night with, including a cat of nine tails which will be made of glass, metal, bones, and stones all connected to a whip. They will beat you unmercifully all night ripping the flesh off your bones. In the midst of all this you shall not utter a word. On the next day you will be brutally nailed to a wooden cross. They will drive nails through your hands and feet. You will experience pain as no other human flesh has, and ever will. As you hang dying a ruthless death, you will cry out to me your Father, and I will turn my face from you. For the sins of all mankind will rest upon you. My son will you do this for me, and save mankind?" "Yes Father, because I love you, and I love our creation."

***<u>Love</u> is God and God is love.

Love encompasses all the attributes of God. Nothing can be counted worthy of any report if true love is not at the core. It is because of love that you exist. In order to get any response from God, you must be operating in love. 1st John 4:8 says, *"He that loves not, knows not God, for God is love."* All the fruits of the Spirit flow from love. It has been said that money makes the world go round, but that is not true. Love is what causes all things to perpetuate. No word, or laws, or any such thing in the bible matters without love. The greatest of all commandments is to love. To operate in love you must walk in the Spirit of God. The flesh only attends to its desires, and does not wish for any good to transpire. **When you are not growing in love, you are growing in the flesh**. Love is attendant to the needs of others. We prove our love to God by loving others. 1st John 4:11-12 says, *"beloved if God so loves us we ought also to love one another. No man hath seen God at anytime if we love one another God dwells in us, and his love is perfected in us."* *Without love you cannot relate to God in anyway. *Without love you cannot obtain the blessing of God on earth, nor can you obtain the Kingdom of Heaven. The opposite of love is anything not in agreement to the Spirit of God.

***Love cannot exist in the midst of impure intentions...

Romans 12:9 says, *"let love be without dissimulation, abhor that which is evil, and cleave to that which is good."* The word dissimulation means to hide ones true feelings. God knows the intentions of the heart. Before love can be set in motion to flow freely in you, you must confess any hidden sin, and forgive those who hurt you. It is not easy to forgive someone who hurt you deeply, and purposely. There is only one way to forgive that person, and it is see them through the eyes that God saw you when you did wrong. *When real love enters, all ill intentions leave.

***The power of love...

Love is so powerful that it has no risking; meaning that it will and can do anything, because it only desires to see the best results for you. For instance when God the Father sent Jesus, He was not taking a risk or a chance, because He did it through and by love, and love can never fail. Whenever you act in love you will always succeed.

* Love is so powerful it can hide you when

101

you are wrong. 1st Peter says, *"Love shall cover a multitude of sins."* Love removes these works of the flesh: un forgiveness, jealousy, envy, gossip, rage, filthy communication, fornication, adultery, stealing, murder, disobedience, evil thinking, and lying. It brings these attributes to life within you; peace, joy, gentleness, meekness, happiness, longsuffering, patience, and kindness.

*You can only possess true love by keeping the commandments of God. Real love reveals itself, and cannot be concealed. When you possess love you will no longer be fearful of things to come. You will have the confidence, knowing that your heart is in right standing. 1st John 4:18 says, *"there is no fear in love: but perfect love casteth out fear because fear hath torment. He that feareth is not made perfect in love."* Perfect love is the way God loves His creation, and we are to emulate that towards each other.

***Sin separates us from God, but does not separate us from God's love

God's love is never ending. It continues to pull us in even when we do wrong. The problem is not with

God's love for us, it is with our lack of commitment to love God in spite of circumstances. Romans 8:38 says, *"I am persuaded that neither death nor life nor angels nor principalities nor powers nor things present nor things to come nor height nor depth nor any other creature shall be able to separate us from the love of God."* Paul was determined to let nothing in existence come between him and God. You must love God more than anything, and anyone. It is because of God that all things were made. God gave us everything that we have. Don't be, or become passionate about creation, but be passionate about the creator. When you began to love and trust in things, and man more than your Father in heaven, your fall has already begun. Nothing or no one has the ability to give life, so how can they or it be worth your eternal life.

*CQ: How do I know if someone truly loves me?
Love is not deceptive or self fulfilling, it is other building. The premier way to determine rather or not someone sincerely loves you is dependant upon what are they willing to part with in order to fulfill your needs, and desires. Jesus was willing to part

with his life for mankind's benefit. Whatever he or she is parting with *for you* must be beneficial to **them.** Also, if a person claims they love you, they will not try and persuade you to do anything against your moral standard of living. The person who truly loves you, loves and fears God first.

***If you love God, you will not knowingly and willfully sin…

John 14:15 says, *"if you love me keep my commandments."* When you consciously break God's laws you are clearly saying that you do not love Him. There is a distinct difference between premeditated sin, and a lapse of character. The problem is that some lapses can turn out to be deadly. Many times you will feel you can do something and God will not recognize what you're doing, but He does. Just because you don't feel or see Him, He's there. Mercifully God's grace covers you even when you are wrong, and not considering Him. Think of the times you were doing wrong and you knew you were wrong but did not reap the repercussions of your wrong doing. Don't continue to lie to yourself and to God by saying that you love

Him; while intentionally doing the opposite of His will. Jesus said the truth will set you free. I came to the point in my personal walk where I confessed before the Lord "I don't love you God", and it was at that point that I was released to walk in liberty and loving God freely. It is not what you say that moves God, it is what you do. **What you do is the proof of how you feel.**

*** Love sacrifices!

The word love and charity are interchangeable. John 3:16 says, *"for God so loved the world that he **gave** his only begotten Son."* Key word in this passage is, gave. You can say you love God, but love is an action word. Saying you love someone means nothing, its only sound and air. A key way to show your love is by giving which defines charity. If your spouse showered you with; love, affection, attention, gifts, and faithfulness, wouldn't that mean more than them only saying over and over I love you, but they're never around. Which would you prefer? I'm glad Jesus didn't look down and say, "hey I love ya'll." But instead He came and showed the greatest display of love till this day and forevermore. Jesus gave His all so we could obtain all. It is true that Abraham acted in faith and obedience when he was heading to sacrifice his son Isaac; but look at the display of love and commitment to God that Abraham possessed. He was willing to sacrifice his son to please God. If the Spirit told you to give your only means of transportation away and ride the bus, would you do it? It will never be what you are sacrificing that matters to God, but the fact that you are willing to sacrifice and obey God in all things. *Love takes away from itself to progress someone else.

***Love only sees the best in a person and always forgives...

1st Peter 4:8 says, *"and above all things have fervent love among yourselves for love shall cover a multitude of sins."* You must be merciful and have a compassionate heart towards everyone. Bitterness and resentment ultimately creates hate. Hate produces death. Quickly identify the spirits you are operating in, and with the name of Jesus, and the power of the Holy Spirit that God gave you, rebuke any evil conscience immediately. Your heart will always tell you when you are wrong. Don't let sin multiply, kill it from the root with the name of Jesus.

When you constantly reflect on God's unconditional love for you, it is hard to see and judge the fought in others. Do love yourself, but not because you've done anything good in life, but because you are God's ultimate creation. You are a literal child of God, and He loves you more than any man can think of loving you. The same love you have for yourself is the same you should have for one another. Paul described it precisely in 1st Corinthians 13:4-7 when he wrote, *"love suffers long and is kind, love envy's not, love boast not itself, it is not puffed up, love doesn't behave itself unseemly, love seeks not it's own, love is not easily provoked, love thinks no evil, love rejoices in truth, love bears all things, and believes all things, love hopes all things."* These are the elements that make up love, now let love create these elements in you. Colossians 3:14 says, *and above all these things put on love, which is the bond of perfection."* It is no surprise that love is the key ingredient which culminates all the other elements prior reviewed.

None of the other steps are effective without the working of love within them.

"On Eagles Wings"

Before I wrote this book I was just coming off a
seven year merry go round in my life. I was totally
discombobulated. The Holy Spirit revealed in my
heart that though I may feel hopeless and confused,
there remained an opportunity for my redemption,
simply because I was still breathing. More
shockingly it was also revealed to me that I can live
in total success, and victory. I believe that the
cockiest statement that can ever be made is for
some one to say "I am perfect." The startling truth
is, perfection is obtainable. The catch, for lack of a
better word is; it will be the hardest thing you will
ever attempt to do. This type of total victory can
only perpetuate by faith through the Holy Spirit.
Perfection can be possessed for short periods of
time by mortal beings like you and me. We must
practice duplicating these times, and shortening any
lapses. I boldly say it is not impossible to be perfect,
only improbable. Your flesh will always be a
hindrance to your spirit man. The flesh can only be
consistently defeated, by constantly starving it from
its vile desires. In all commonality the natural body

was designed and created by God, and must be given nourishment and not be deprived from its basic needs in order to survive and progress. The problem arrives when we give the flesh what it wants instead of what it needs. There is no questioning the fact, that there is a battle that takes place within the body of every person. The battle is between good and evil. It will remain a battle until you choose to surrender to one of the sides. God is not in a fight with Satan. Satan is in a fight with you. You begin to win the fight the moment you surrender to Jesus Christ. Confessing that Jesus is your Lord and King, and surrendering to Jesus are totally different from one another. I have personally fallen many times because I lived my life according to confession, and not in total surrender. After surrendering my existence to the will of God, I activated these elements of victory: faith, diligence, virtue, knowledge, temperance, patience, godliness, brotherly kindness, and love. These are the elements of righteousness and perfection. God reveals Himself through our righteous living.

***Have **faith** in God, knowing that it was faith that has brought you to this point, and it will be by faith that you will achieve the next level

***Be **diligent** in walking by faith and in holiness while seeking God, and His perfect will.

***Be **virtuous** in your livelihood and the decisions you make. Know that you are worth to much to be tainted by sinful hands.

***Seek to have full **knowledge** of God, and constantly be looking to grow in God's Word and knowing His ways.

***Act in **temperance** when faced with any temptation. Practice discipline in all facets of your daily walk, knowing that your destiny is controlled by the decisions you make.

***Have **patience** in order to be made perfect knowing that you have a specific season and purpose that will be released in God's timing. Be in all assurance that your waiting is not in vain, but is for your completion.

***Live in **Godliness** so that you can display the qualities and characteristics of Jesus, remembering that Godly living is the only way you can obtain eternal life.

***Show **brotherly kindness** to all mankind by having mercy and compassion on everyone. Strive towards creating equality among all in society.
*****Love** and forgive those who hurt and hate you because this is the only way to love God, for without love nothing else matters.

2nd Peter 1:10 says, *"For if ye do these things,* **ye shall never fall."** The power to be totally victorious was given to us when Jesus commandeered it for me and you His children on resurrection day. To demonstrate the elements of victory as stated above you must walk in the Spirit. Satan indeed scored a temporal victory when he deceived man in the garden, but God mercifully devised a plan of redemption. In God's reconstructed plan for mankind He gave us power over Satan, and all things pertaining to him. My, my how the tables have turned. Satan can only hope that you will give in to his many temptations, and choose him over Jesus and eternal life. Every time you are tempted you are given a choice to choose Jesus and eternal life, or Satan and eternal damnation. Satan is a proven miserable foe, and it is true "misery loves company." You must choose what life you want to live. All the keys to success dwell in the Word of God; which is why it says. *"let the word of Christ dwell in you richly"* (Colossians 3:16). God gave us the ability, and it is His desire for the entire creation to walk in perfect health, wealth, happiness, fellowship, and love.

    * The eagle is the most protuberant of birds. It is best known for its keen sight, majestic style of soaring, and strength. The eagle has been used by governments and militaries to symbolize authority for many centuries. The Word of God uses the phrase "they shall mount up with eagle's wings." You must take this statement literally to heart, knowing that we are above the ways of Satan, and this world. *"You're a chosen generation, a royal priesthood, a holy nation"* (1st Peter 2:9)! You're the best of the best! You are God's specific creation designed in His likeness. Don't belittle yourself and compromise to the degradation and apathy of sin. The eagle can soar for long periods without flapping his wings one time, and with one flap he can elevate his flight by many feet. The eagle has this unique ability because he is a creation who is under God's

provision. What more are we, seeing that we are His children. We have the same abilities to fly high above failure without working profusely hard because God is with, and in us. God has given His creation the power to overcome all hindrances, but this power must be expressly demonstrated by way of the Word, through the Holy Spirit, unto God the Father.

***Jude verse 24 says, *"**Now unto him that is able to keep you from falling and to present you faultless before the presence of his glory with exceeding joy.**"*

To be continued…

www.ingramcontent.com/pod-product-compliance
Lightning Source LLC
LaVergne TN
LVHW091158080426
835509LV00006B/744